My First
German
Lesson
Color & Learn!

Illustrated by
Roz Fulcher

Ich liebe Dich.
ikh **lee**-beh dich

Dover Publications, Inc.
Mineola, New York

This handy book will have you speaking German in no time! More than sixty illustrated pages include commonly used words and phrases in both German and English. Below each German word or phrase you'll find its pronunciation. A syllable that is **boldfaced** should be stressed.

Whether it's just for fun, for travel, or to have a conversation with a friend or relative, you'll find out how to talk about the weather, tell what you'd like at mealtime, and many other helpful phrases—and you can color while you learn!

Bibliographical Note

This Dover edition, first published in 2019, is a republication in a different format of the work originally published by Dover in 2015 as *Color & Learn Easy German Phrases for Kids*.

International Standard Book Number

ISBN-13: 978-0-486-83310-1
ISBN-10: 0-486-83310-0

Manufactured in the United States by LSC Communications
83310001   2019
www.doverpublications.com

1

See you later.

What's your name?

Das ist
dahss isst

1. *meine Mutter*
my-neh **moot**-tair

2. *mein Vater*
myn fah-tair

3. *meine Schwester*
my-neh **shvess**-tair

4. *mein Bruder*
myn broo-dair

This is my   **1. Mother**   **2. Father**
             3. Sister   **4. Brother**

How old are you?

    I am _____ years old.

I'm allergic to nuts/eggs.

I love you.

What's for breakfast?   1. Cereal

2. Toast
tohst

3. Eier
eye-air

2. Toast   3. Eggs

It's time for lunch. I want. . .

1. a sandwich

2. Joghurt
yohk-urt

3. einen Hamburger
eye-nen **hem**-boor-ger

2. Yogurt   3. Hamburger

I'm hungry! What's for dinner?

1. Huhn?
hoon

2. Fisch?
fish

3. Pizza?
pih-tzah

1. Chicken?   2. Fish?   3. Pizza?

What's for dessert?

1. Eis
eyss

2. Obst
ohpst

3. Plätzchen
pletts-chenn

1. Ice cream   2. Fruit
3. Cookies

4. *fahrrad fahren*
fahr-raht **fahr**-enn

3. *zeichnen*
tsych-nenn

3. Draw   4. Bike

1. I'm sorry. 2. Don't worry.
3. It's okay.

20

Can you help me, please? I'm lost.

Frohe Weihnachten!

froh-eh **vy**-nahkh-tenn

Merry Christmas!

Glückliches neues Jahr!

glook-lich-ess **noy**-ess **yahr**

Happy New Year!

This is delicious! I'd like some more.

Where are you from?
I am from _____.

die Tage der Woche

dee **tah**-geh dair **vaw**-keh

Monday *Montag*
mohn-tahk

Tuesday *Dienstag*
deens-tahk

Wednesday *Mittwoch*
mitt-vawch

Days of the week

Thursday *Donnerstag*
dunn-airs-tahk

Friday *Freitag*
fry-tahk

Saturday *Samstag*
zahmss-tahk

Sunday *Sonntag*
zunn-tahk

die Monate
dee **moh**-nah-teh

January

Januar
yahnn-oo-arr

February

Februar
fay-broo-arr

March

März
mehrts

April

April
ah-**prill**

May

Mai
my

June

Juni
yoo-nee

Months

Juli
yoo-lee

August
ow-**goost**

September
sepp-**temm**-bair

Oktober
awk-**toh**-bair

November
no-**vemm**-bair

Dezember
day-**tsemm**-bair

die Nummern
dee **noom**-airn

eins
eynss

zwei
zwye

drei
dry

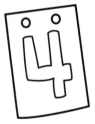

vier
feer

fünf
foonff

Numbers

sechs
zekss

sieben
zee-benn

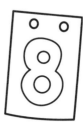

acht
achtt

neun
noyn

zehn
tsayn

die Farben
dee **fahr**-benn

Green
Grün
groon

Red
Rot
roht

Blue
Blau
blow (like "how")

Colors

Yellow
Gelb
gellp

Colors

White
Weiß
vyss

Black
Shvartz
shvahrts

Orange
Orange
oh-**rahng**-zhuh

Purple
Purpurrot
poor-poor-ote

Gray
Grau
grow (like "cow")

1. Let's go to the park!
2. Awesome idea!

1. How much does it cost?
2. It's one dollar.

Gehen wir am Strand! Ich hole . . .
gay-enn **veer** ahm **shtrahnt!** ikh **hoh**-leh

Let's go to the beach! I will get . . .

1. einen Badeanzug
eye-nenn **bah**-deh-**ahn**-tsook

2. Lotion
loh-tsee-own

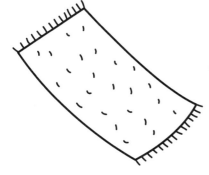

3. ein Handtuch
eyn **hahnt**-tooch

1. my bathing suit   2. my lotion
3. my towel

Please.

It's hot today. I'll wear . . .

1. ein T-Shirt
eyn tee-shirt

2. eine kurze Hose
eye-neh **koor**-tseh **hoh**-zeh

3. Sandalen
zahn-**dahl**-enn

1. a T-shirt 2. shorts
3. sandals

1. einen Schal
eye-nenn **shahll**

2. Handschuhe
hahnnt-shoo-eh

3. Stiefel
shtee-fell

4. einen Mantel
eye-nenn **mahn**-tell

1. my scarf
2. my gloves
3. my boots
4. my coat

1. einen Pullover
eye-nen puhl-**oh**-ver

2. eine Decke
eye-ne **deck**-eh

3. eine Jacke
eye-ne **yah**-keh

1. a sweater   2. a blanket
3. a jacket

Do you speak English?

Sorry, I don't understand.

I'm thirsty. I want . . .

1. Wasser
vah-sair

2. Saft
zahftt

3. Milch
milkh

1. water   2. juice   3. milk

Excuse me. Where is the nearest . . .

1. das näheste Restaurant?
dahss **nay**-ess-teh ress-toh-**rahnn**

2. die näheste Bushaltestelle?
dee **nay**-ess-teh **buss**-hahl-teh-**stell**-eh?

3. die näheste U-Bahn?
dee **nay**-ess-teh **oo**-bahnn

1. restaurant?   2. bus stop?
3. subway?

Do you have a pet?   I have . . .

*1. einen
Hund*
eye-nen
hoondt

*2. eine
Katze*
eye-neh
kaht-zeh

3. einen Fisch
eye-nen fish

4. einen Vogel
eye-nen **foh**-gell

5. einen Hamster
eye-nen **hamm**-stair

1. a dog   2. a cat   3. a fish
4. a bird   5. a hamster

1. *Fernsehen gucken?*
fairn-zay-enn **ghook**-enn

2. *ins Kino gehen?*
ints **kee**-noh **gay**-enn

3. *nach draußen gehen?*
nach **drow**-ssen **gay**-enn

Darf ich . . .?
dahrff Ikh

Can I . . . 1. Watch TV?
2. Go to a movie? 3. Go outside?

1. Oma
oh-mah

2. Opa
oh-pah

3. Tante
tahnt-teh

4. Onkel
unn-kell

5. Cousine
koo-**zee**-neh

6. Cousin
koo-**zann**

1. Grandma
2. Grandpa
3. Aunt
4. Uncle
5. Cousin (girl)
6. Cousin (boy)

61

Good night.